Return to D-Day
35 Men, 70 Landings at Normandy

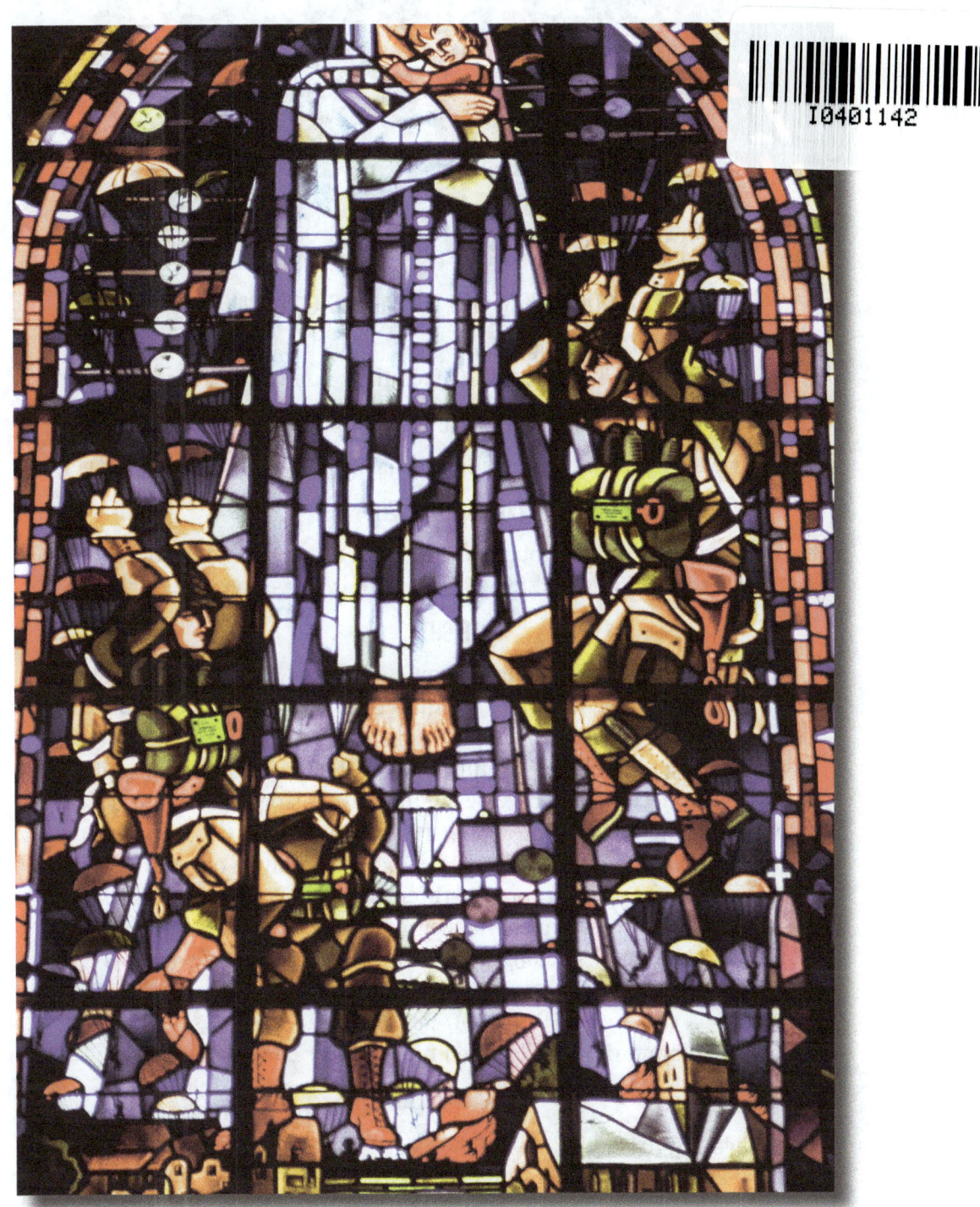

RETURN TO D-DAY: 35 MEN, 70 LANDINGS AT NORMANDY

A Warriors Publishing Group book published by arrangement with The Greatest Generations Foundation

PRINTING HISTORY

Warriors Publishing Group edition/June 2014. All rights reserved.

COPYRIGHT © 2014

by Warriors Publishing Group and The Greatest Generations Foundation
Cover art copyright © 2014 by Gerry Kissell gerrykissell.com

RIGHTS

All rights reserved under International and Pan-American Copyright Conventions. By payment of the required fees, you have been granted the non-exclusive, non-transferable right to access and read the text of this ebook onscreen. No part of this text may be reproduced, transmitted, downloaded, decompiled, reverse engineered, or stored in or introduced into any information storage and retrieval system, in any form or by any means, whether electronic or mechanical, now known or hereinafter invented, without the express written permission of the publisher.
The name "Warriors Publishing Group" and the logo
are trademarks belonging to Warriors Publishing Group

ISBN 978-0-9897983-2-7
Library of Congress Control Number: 2014904848

IMAGE CREDITS

All images provided by The Greatest Generations Foundation, and all rights belong to them. Credit for all veteran return photos: John Riedy.
www.johnriedy.com

DEDICATION

Over the years that The Greatest Generations Foundation has been privileged to accompany World War II veterans on emotional returns to the distant battlefields where much of their youth was sacrificed in service to our nation, we have learned about service, sacrifice and selfless devotion to duty. Most of all we have learned that there is no greater love than that shown by a man who is willing to lay down his life for his friends. In that spirit and with profound respect for all that lost their lives in war, this book is proudly dedicated.

FOREWORD

BY CAPT. DALE A. DYE, USMC (RET.)

It was just a rock, flat and slightly oval, completely nondescript except for its color. Of all the rocks on that blustery French beach, this one caught my eye and halted my stroll for long moments as I stared at it. It was a rusty red, a color familiar to me from other distant battlefields.

"Pretty rock," the old man said in a tone hushed by the hiss of Atlantic surf and a certain reverence for where we were on that day in early June.

"Guess so…" I followed his gaze out to the horizon where he seemed to see something I could not. "It just reminded me of something."

The old man adjusted the thick lenses he required to see after 80 years of watching the world spin through war and peace, staring once again at the rock amid the sands of Omaha Beach. "Dried blood," he grunted. "Could be mine. I landed right near here. Got hit at the high-water mark; never made it off the beach."

The incident stayed with me for the remainder of the day I spent walking Omaha and Utah Beaches with a group of World War II veterans who had soldiered on or over those bloody sands back in June 1944. For several days prior to the beach walk, I'd listened quietly, in a constant state of awe, as they related their stories of what they'd seen, done, or suffered on that day when Allied forces finally cracked Hitler's stranglehold on the continent and pushed on to liberate the people of Nazi-occupied Europe. There was always a tint of humor in the stories, a certain self-deprecating attitude about their individual efforts on that crucial day in the bloody history of World War II, but the common intensity of their reflections was almost palpable.

Pressed for details, the old soldiers, sailors, and airmen who fought on D-Day would often tell me they couldn't remember one detail or another. "It was a long time ago," most would say. And then they would proceed to relate the most intimate and personal feelings and impressions they still carried from that infamous day. "If there was ever a seminal experience in my life," said one old 1st Infantry Division trooper, a rare survivor of the first wave to land at Omaha Beach who went on to become a college professor, "that was it. Everything changed forever because of that experience. I was never able to look at life the same way after D-Day."

All of his fellow veterans agreed on that point if not much else as they caroused, remembered, and re-visited the places where their lives changed forever. And they were all devoutly grateful for the chance to tour the place where the change took place. In a strange way, all seemed to view the visit like someone who has been gone for a long time and found himself back in his hometown, walking around and remembering the places where he was born and raised. "That's it exactly," said one of the veterans who had been shot out of his landing craft on the approach to Utah Beach. "You could say I was born on that beach. I was one man before D-Day and another man entirely after that."

"The guy who said you can never go home again had it right," the rifleman turned college teacher commented as he stared at a museum manikin garbed in the same uniform and carrying the same weapon he remembered from his days as a soldier. "You go through something like war and nothing is ever the same again. It's hard to believe it can change a man the way it does, and maybe that's why I came back here—just to recall how that kind of change happened."

It was author Thomas Wolfe who expressed the sentiment in the title of his 1940 novel, "You Can't Go Home Again." After the D-Day visit with those old veterans, I re-read Wolfe's book and found what he—and those old veterans—meant concerning life-changing events. "You can't go back home to your family, back home to your childhood," Wolfe wrote, "back home to the old forms and systems of things that once seemed everlasting…" The author said something else that would make a fitting epitaph for any of those old soldiers and for combat veterans who survive other wars:

> *"This is a man, who, if he can remember ten golden moments of joy and happiness out of all his years, ten moments unmarked by care, unseamed by aches or itches, has power to lift himself with his expiring breath and say: I have lived upon this earth and known glory!"*

ABOUT THE GREATEST GENERATIONS FOUNDATION

Most of the men and women who fought in World War II have never been back. Seventy years ago, they followed orders and put their lives on the line. They saw adventure as well as horrors, and left many friends behind. Those who survived came home. They built lives and families and careers. Many are now facing their final journey.

The Greatest Generations Foundation wants to make sure they don't leave without the chance to visit that chapter in their histories. Without walking once again on the beaches of Normandy or the island of Iwo Jima. Without feeling some closure and peace. The Greatest Generations Foundation wants to make sure they have a chance to tell their stories. Their stories are, after all, about a defining episode in our history and the history of the world. They are stories that can and should be preserved.

The Greatest Generations Foundation is a charitable organization dedicated to serving war veterans. Our mission is to promote recognition and respect for U.S. and allied war veterans while enhancing historical education for today's youth. We work to make sure that the dedication and bravery of these veterans is never forgotten, nor that the value of their deeds be allowed to disappear into history.

The Greatest Generations Foundation
Remember Those Who Served

www.tggf.org

RETURN TO D-DAY
HEADQUARTERS:

Planning for Operation Overlord—the D-Day 1944 invasion of Nazi-occupied Europe—was primarily done by U.S. General Dwight D. Eisenhower and his staff at Supreme Headquarters Allied Expeditionary Force (SHAEF) in England. SHAEF remained in the United Kingdom until sufficient troops were landed on the continent, at which point a forward headquarters was established in France. The closely guarded buildings and grounds were located at Bushy Park, Teddington in London from December 1943 until the end of the war. An adjacent street named SHAEF Way remains a London landmark.

Second Lieutenant Lloyd Falk USAAF
Meteorologist
8th U.S. Air Force and Supreme Headquarters Allied Expeditionary Force

After he was drafted into military service in July 1942, Lloyd took basic training in Florida and then was assigned to technical school at Lowry Field in Colorado where he learned to maintain and repair the top-secret Norden bombsight, the instrument used in American bombers to aim precision drops on enemy targets. After a while, Lloyd decided he wanted to become an officer and applied for acceptance at a cadet school, where he could train to become an Army Air Corps meteorologist. He received technical training in the field at Grand Rapids, Michigan and was commissioned a second lieutenant when he graduated in 1943. Shortly thereafter, he was on his way across the Atlantic for duty as a weather forecaster with the 8th Air Force. The call for trained meteorologists was heavy as allied bombers were fighting daily battles with inclement weather at English bases and over enemy targets in Nazi-occupied Europe.

After arriving in England for some further training in the British weather reporting system, Lt. Falk was assigned to an 8th Air Force bomber base in East Anglia. He wasn't there long before orders arrived sending him to Supreme Headquarters Allied Expeditionary Force (SHAEF) at Teddington. He became a member of a small, elite meteorological team that compiled weather data and provided forecast briefings to General Dwight Eisenhower and his staff who were planning the invasion landings in Normandy. His particular duty was to provide forecasts for upper altitude wind conditions required to plan bombing missions in support of the D-Day invasion. He remained with SHAEF for the rest of the war in England and then in France.

In 2012, Lloyd returned to the American cemetery at Normandy, which is dedicated to American lives lost during World War II. He immediately spotted a specific grave and approached it, carrying a large rock he had taken from a pile of rubble and runway remains at Thorpe Abbotts Bomb Base. Lloyd placed the rock on top of the marker—a Star of David—in the Jewish tradition. He said, "I did not know this man, but I know he was Jewish from the Star of David."

He gave this token to a fallen brother because he knew that soldier's family was far away and would not easily make a trip out to place a rock.

RETURN TO D-DAY
PATHFINDERS:

The American and British airborne portion of the Normandy landings was called Operation Neptune. Prior to the arrival of larger units of parachutists, each airborne division sent Pathfinders ahead to jump in and scout the area. These volunteer soldiers were the first ones on the ground where they established visual and electronic beacons to guide the airborne armada onto designated landing zones.

Staff Sergeant William Hannigan USA
Pathfinder
Headquarters Company, 508th Parachute Infantry Regiment
82nd Airborne Division
VII Corps

35 MEN, 70 LANDINGS AT NORMANDY

Bill Hannigan served in combat with the 3rd Platoon, Company H, 504th Parachute Infantry Regiment of the 82nd Airborne Division in North Africa and Italy before he moved with that unit to England and a period of intense preparation for the airborne phase of the D-Day landings. His unit had been chewed up badly during the fighting at Anzio which left only 30 survivors in his rifle company. Other rifle companies of the regiment were in similarly bad shape so the plan was to leave the 504th PIR out of the airborne assault on Normandy and keep them as a reserve force in England.

When Bill found out about that he began to search for a way to get more directly involved in one of the most pivotal operations of the war. A sister unit—the 508th Parachute Regiment—was looking for experienced jumpers to land as Pathfinders and Bill volunteered. He landed in Normandy before the main body of the 508th PIR jumped in the early hours of D-Day. During those deadly first hours on the ground, Bill lost his best friend Joe Burns who was killed in action. He went on to fight through the hedgerows with his adopted unit and then returned to his parent 504th PIR.

After a period of rest and reorganization in England, Bill made the jump into Holland for Operation Market Garden. He was with the 504th PIR during the assault crossing of the Waal River at Nijmegen, one of the most daring and deadly actions of the war. He also fought through the Siegfried Line and in the Battle of the Bulge, the last desperate enemy push to regain lost ground.

RETURN TO D-DAY

First Lieutenant Roy M. Hanna USA
Pathfinder
Headquarters Company, 508th Parachute Infantry Regiment
82nd Airborne Division
VII Corps

Roy Hanna was a combat veteran from campaigns in North Africa, Italy, and Sicily where he served as a machinegun platoon leader when his unit was sent to England for rest and replacements in 1944. Because of the casualties and battle-damage the 504th PIR had suffered in previous campaigns a high-level decision was made to exclude Roy's outfit from the D-Day jump. That didn't sit well with him, so when Roy discovered other regiments of the 82nd were looking for people to jump into Normandy as Pathfinders, he volunteered. Everyone knew that Operation Overlord was going to be a major event in the war effort and Roy was determined to be part of it. With some other volunteers from the 504th, Roy was accepted to jump before with main body of paratroopers as a Pathfinder for the 508th PIR.

He made the jump carrying special radio gear that was designed to guide the following waves of C-47s to their designated drop zones. It was an ordeal from the start with the Pathfinders jumping into areas that had been flooded by the Germans but Roy managed to survive and helped to set up the guidance system for the paratroops that would follow. He spent the next weeks fighting with the 82nd through stiff German resistance and counterattacks in the Normandy hedgerows. When the division was eventually pulled out of the combat zone and returned to England, Roy rejoined his parent unit and jumped with them into Holland for Operation Market Garden. He fought with the 504th PIR through Belgium and other battlefields of central Europe until the war ended.

His return to France more than a half-century later with fellow D-Day veterans was an emotional time for Roy. "In many ways, it defined who we were and why we were there," he said, "which was to defeat an enemy and help liberate people from the tyranny of Nazism." During his trip, a man he met showed him an old photograph. It showed a little girl smiling between Hanna and another soldier somewhere in 1944. On the back the man had written that it was a picture of his daughter "with my two heroes who gave us the gift of freedom." That moment, looking at that fading photo, meant as much to Roy Hanna as any of the many medals he was awarded for his service in World War II.

RETURN TO D-DAY
PARATROOPS:

To deter enemy counter-attacks and to seize vital objectives inland from the D-Day landing beaches, the Allies staged pre-dawn jumps by some 24,000 paratroopers. They were followed by daylight glider missions carrying airborne infantry to support the paratroops. The spearhead units were the American 82nd and 101st Airborne Divisions and the U.K. 6th Airborne Division composed of British and Canadian paratroops.

Private Alvin R. Henderson USA
Rifleman and Former Prisoner of War
501st Parachute Infantry Regiment
101st Airborne Division
VII Corps

Private Alvin R. Henderson was a volunteer for the parachute infantry when he completed his basic training. He joined the Screaming Eagles of the elite 101st Airborne Division for service in the European Theater of Operations and was assigned to the 501st Parachute Infantry Regiment designated as one of the first units to jump on D-Day. After an intense period of training in England, the 501st PIR took off in a huge formation of C-47 aircraft on the evening of June 5, 1944 and headed for France. They flew across the English Channel in pitch dark and jumped into combat five hours before the amphibious landings were scheduled to begin on the Normandy beaches. The aircraft carrying Alvin and his fellow paratroopers were widely scattered due to a combination of low clouds, poor visibility and enemy anti-aircraft fire, but the 501st managed to make landing zones north and east of the enemy-held city of Carentan, where they were immediately involved in intense combat with German defenders. Things did not go as planned, but because the paratroopers were well prepared, trained, and rehearsed, the regiment accomplished its multiple missions.

After a period of rest and retraining in England, Alvin returned with his unit to make the parachute assault into Holland for Operation Market Garden. During the fighting there, he walked into a German ambush and was captured. He spent the remainder of the war as a POW.

When many years later, Alvin attended a reunion of the 101st, no one there recognized him. When he told them his name, shocked faces looked back at him—they thought he had died during Market Garden. During his return to Normandy in 2010, Alvin spoke about having a clear conscience about the war. He said, "Every day when I shave, I can look in the mirror and know I did what I was supposed to do."

Staff Sergeant Harry D. Zimmerman USA
Rifleman
Headquarters, 508th Parachute Infantry Regiment
82nd Airborne Division
VII Corps

Harry Zimmerman was a veteran paratrooper before he made the jump with the 508th PIR on D-Day. Serving with the 504th PIR, he had already experienced war first hand as a .30 caliber machinegunner in North Africa and made his first combat jump during the invasion of Sicily. During that operation, he was cut off from his unit and spent three days on his own, dodging and fighting German troops before he rejoined his outfit. He made the landings on the bloody beaches of Anzio before his unit was pulled out of combat to prepare for D-Day.

Attached to the 508th PIR for the Normandy operation, Harry made the jump on D-Day where well-rehearsed plans started to come apart rapidly. Clouds and heavy anti-aircraft fire caused the formations of C-47s to break up and many of the planes strayed off course. This situation was made worse by the unexpected presence of German units in many of the designated landing areas. These enemy formations kept Pathfinders from setting up their guidance signals and caused many of the pilots to overshoot assigned drop zones. Harry made it safely to the ground after a turbulent bail-out and landing in a marshy area inland of the landing beaches where he scrambled to help find and organize scattered paratroopers. The 508th was assigned to secure the southwestern portion of the 82nd Airborne Divisions' sector with responsibility for capturing and holding two vital bridges over the Douve River. Scattered units finally mustered along a main railroad line and began their assault to seize and hold the bridges.

After D-Day and the subsequent brutal fighting in the Normandy hedgerows, Harry made another combat jump with his unit in Holland for Operation Market Garden. He went on to fight in the bloody crossing of the Nijmegen Bridge. He was also involved in the Battle of the Bulge and other campaigns throughout Central Europe.

RETURN TO D-DAY

Staff Sergeant Albert Mampre
Combat Medic
506th Parachute Infantry Regiment
101st Airborne Division
VII Corps

As a volunteer for airborne duty, Albert was initially trained at Camp Taccoa, Georgia where he was assigned to the 506th Parachute Infantry Regiment, a part of the 101st Airborne Division. When the unit was properly formed and trained in infantry tactics, they were sent to Fort Benning, Georgia for parachute training. Albert completed his jumps and then headed overseas as a combat medic with the famous "Band Of Brothers" of Company E, 506th PIR. He made the jump into Normandy on D-Day and was involved in heavy combat in the hedgerows inland of the landing beaches. He was eventually promoted to Staff Sergeant and placed in charge of all the medics in the second battalion of the 506th PIR.

When the 101st Airborne Division was alerted for the Market Garden operation in enemy-occupied Holland in September 1944, Albert Mampre also made that jump and landed with his unit near Son. Surviving intense combat during that operation, he continued to serve with his unit and was with the 506th PIR when they were rushed to Bastogne to stop the enemy surprise attack that became known as The Battle of the Bulge. Through one of the most intense, frigid winters of the entire war, Mampre continued to supervise medics and save lives until his unit was relieved following the successful stand against the German assault. Staff Sergeant Albert Mampre was with his unit at Hitler's Eagles Nest (*Berchtesgaden*) when the war ended.

Private John Cipolla USA
Rifleman
501st Parachute Infantry Regiment
101st Airborne Division
VII Corps

As a rifleman with Company C, 1st Battalion, 501st Parachute Infantry Regiment, John Cipolla jumped into Nazi-occupied France six hours before the landings were scheduled to begin on the Normandy Beaches. Due to combinations of wind, weather, darkness and enemy ground fire, the C-47s carrying the two American Airborne Divisions (101st and 82nd) were scattered and many of the troopers dropped outside their intended landing zones. This was especially dangerous for John and other paratroopers of the Screaming Eagles who landed in many areas that the Germans had flooded to disrupt just such a landing attempt. Shortly after 1:30 on the morning of D-Day, John landed in one of these marshy areas near the Normandy town of Ste-Mère-Église. He was isolated and alone for some time but kept moving in the direction he knew lead to his unit's objective. He encountered other lost paratroopers and used the toy cricket issued to all 101st paratroopers to identify himself to friendly forces. Joe eventually joined up with other stragglers and they moved out in an effort to find a larger outfit encountering small units of confused German soldiers along the way. In the dark before dawn on D-Day, Joe and some other paratroopers broke into a French house where a family was hiding in confusion about what was happening on that June morning. The French family was overjoyed when they realized their visitors were American soldiers and not Germans.

Joe finally found C Company the next day and fought with them through the Normandy campaign involving routing German defenders from fortified hedgerows. Along the way he helped liberate several French towns including Ste-Mère-Église and St-Côme-du-Mont. He survived the campaign and returned with his unit to England for rest and reorganization. He was in England for about four weeks before his unit was alerted for a jump into Holland on Operation Market Garden. At one point on that operation, he was hit in the face by shrapnel and mistaken for dead by the medics. He corrected that error and survived to return home at the end of the war.

During Joe's return to Normandy, he remarked to a student also on the trip, "Do not focus on the bad things. Put them out of your mind and continue having a good time like we have been."

RETURN TO D-DAY

Private First Class Wilson Colwell USA
Rifleman
502ⁿᵈ Parachute Infantry Regiment
101ˢᵗ Airborne Division
VII Corps

Wilson Colwell dropped out of school during World War II and joined the army at age 15 hoping to qualify for pilot training. The Army Air Corps wasn't taking any pilot trainees who hadn't graduated from high school, so Wilson decided that if he couldn't fly airplanes, he could surely jump out of them. He volunteered for training as a paratrooper. After infantry training and jump school, he joined the Screaming Eagles of the 101st Airborne Division and headed for the European Theater of Operations. After a period of hectic training and top-secret preparations, the airborne invasion was launched in the dark on June 5, 1944. Bill was just 16 years old when he jumped over Normandy.

The 502nd PIR took off at night out of British air bases at Membury and Greenham Common in the first wave of paratroopers to depart for Nazi-occupied Europe. They were headed for drop zones inland from the Utah landing beach with the mission of seizing two northern causeways over a river in Normandy that had to be held for crossing by the infantry and armor expected to advance from Utah Beach. The regiment's mission also included destroying a battery of German heavy artillery that threatened the landing beaches. Bill fought with his unit to accomplish each of these vital missions serving primarily as a scout and reconnoitering enemy positions as his company advanced. He survived the vicious hedgerow fighting in Normandy and returned to England where his unit was rested and re-equipped for a proposed jump into Holland as part of Operation Market Garden. Bill made that jump and fought with his unit across the rest of Europe including operations in Belgium and the Rhineland. He was wounded and hospitalized during this combat but returned to his unit in time to fight in the Battle of the Bulge where he stood with his unit against heavy German pressure at Bastogne.

During his return to Normandy, the group visited the Brittany American Cemetery, which is home to some 4,000 American heroes. The men said that it was just luck that they did not end up under a cross or on a wall of the missing. Colwell says it was because he had a praying mother—and believes God was watching over him.

RETURN TO D-DAY

Corporal Leslie Harris USA
Squad Leader
501st Parachute Infantry Regiment
101st Airborne Division
VII Corps

Leslie Harris completed airborne training at Fort Benning, Georgia and graduated into service as a paratrooper with the Screaming Eagles of the 101st Airborne Division. Assigned to the veteran 501st Parachute Infantry Regiment, Leslie was with his unit during prolonged training maneuvers in North Carolina, Tennessee, and Louisiana until January 1944 when the division was assigned overseas for service in the D-Day landings then being planned.

Jumping out of a plane onto heavily contested soil should be terrifying, but Leslie maintains that he was not scared, because once they were over the Channel, there was no turning back. During his return in 2012, he said, "Lots of men spent the entire time praying, some played cards, and they all told jokes until the door was opened over Normandy."

Leslie's first combat jump on D-Day was a memorable one. He remembers seeing a sky full of red and white tracer fire as he left the C-47 over Normandy. He landed in a swampy area and was soaking wet, struggling with the parachute and equipment when he finally heard the clicking of one of the toy crickets 101st paratroopers had all been issued to help identify each other in the dark. He responded with his own cricket and got a hand getting out of the muck from a friendly paratrooper. Like so many other scattered paratroopers that eventful day in France, Leslie scrambled to find others so they could organize themselves and get on with their vital mission. He survived the horrendous fighting against stubborn German resistance in the Normandy hedgerows before his outfit was taken off the fighting line for rest and reorganization in England.

His next combat jump into Holland on Operation Market Garden was just as memorable. A cousin was flying the plane transporting Leslie and his unit into Holland. He called Leslie up to the cockpit and handed him a .45 caliber pistol, saying his paratrooper cousin was more likely to need it than he was. Leslie was wounded by shrapnel during subsequent combat in Holland but returned to his unit and fought with them across Central Europe until the end of the war.

RETURN TO D-DAY

Private First Class Edward J. Tipper USA
506th Parachute Infantry Regiment
101st Airborne Division
VII Corps

Ed Tipper served as a noncommissioned officer with the famous Easy Company of the 2nd Battalion, 506th Parachute Infantry Regiment. As one of the Band of Brothers, he made his first combat jump into Normandy on D-Day in 1944. Like many other paratroopers that day, he was scattered off the mark by C-47s which were dodging flak and searching for designated landing zones in the dark. Shortly after he got on the ground, Ed found some others from his unit and they were promptly involved in a running firefight with German defenders. He was with his reassembled unit when they made the assault on the heavily-defended Marmion Farm, one of the prime objectives of the D-Day airborne assault.

He went on to fight in the brutal house-to-house clearing operation in Carentan with the Screaming Eagles. During this intense combat, he was badly wounded by an enemy mortar round that destroyed his right eye and broke both of his legs. He was evacuated from the combat zone to a hospital in England where his right eye was removed while he recovered from the rest of his wounds. Unable to continue the fight, Ed Tipper was returned to the United States for further treatment and a medical discharge from active service.

T/5 Ralph K Manley USA
Demolition Man
Headquarters, 501st Parachute Infantry Regiment
101st Airborne Division
VII Corps

35 MEN, 70 LANDINGS AT NORMANDY

Ralph Manley quit high school just before graduation in December 1942 to join the Army and do his part for the allied effort in World War II. After basic training, he volunteered for paratroops and was assigned to the 101st. He underwent advanced training in combat demolitions involving work with dangerous high explosives. Ralph was with the 501st when they boarded troopships in Boston for the trip overseas. After a rough 12-day crossing of the Atlantic, the convoy carrying the Screaming Eagles arrived in England and began training for the impending invasion of Nazi-occupied Europe.

While training in England, Ralph and the other soldiers preparing for D-Day got their first hints about the nature of the war they were about to fight as they observed German "Buzz Bombs" descending on London and other areas of the country. In a movement bound in utmost secrecy, the paratroopers slated to lead the invasion were trucked to airports where they boarded C-47 transports that would carry them to Normandy. As a demolition specialist, Ralph carried a heavy load of high explosives along with his standard equipment. He would use those explosives to destroy enemy defenses and important structures to blast a corridor for troops advancing from the invasion beaches.

Prior to take off for the D-Day jump, Ralph's unit got a special visit from General Dwight Eisenhower, the Supreme Commander of the Allied Expeditionary Forces. The general shook Ralph's hand and said just a few words the young paratrooper would never forget: "You're about to embark on a great crusade and I wish you good luck." Manley says the words made him ready to take on the whole German army single-handedly. When it came time to board the planes, T/5 Ralph Manley had to have help from his buddies. He was carrying a load that brought his body weight up to nearly 400 pounds.

As soon as Manley's plane crossed over the French coast, German anti-aircraft rounds hit the aircraft and he remembers a sky-full of tracer rounds that made it "look like the 4th of July."

Manley's C-47, carrying 18 paratroopers, took several hits and caught fire. He was one of only five paratroopers to successfully jump out of the plane before it crashed. After a rough landing, Manley joined up with other scattered paratroops and spent the next six weeks fighting against stiff German resistance in the Normandy hedgerows. During that ordeal, he earned two Bronze Star Medals and five Purple Hearts for wounds suffered in combat. Ralph Manley doesn't regret a moment of his combat experiences. "The war did not make me bitter," he said. "It made me better, because I have such a deep appreciation for our freedoms."

RETURN TO D-DAY
AIR SUPPORT:

Bombers and fighters from the U.S. 8th and 15th Air Forces and the British Bomber Command played a pivotal role in preparations for the D-Day invasions. Softening up beach defenses and striking vital targets to deter enemy counter-attacks on the landing beaches, Allied airmen suffered significant losses. Between April 1944 when the air offensive over Normandy began and right up until D-Day in June, the Allies flew 14,000 missions losing 12,000 airmen and 2,000 aircraft.

Staff Sergeant Elmer "Lucky" McGinty USAAF
339th Bomb Squadron, 95th Bombardment Group (Heavy)
8th U.S. Air Force

Lucky McGinty flew 29 combat missions in B-17 Flying Fortress bombers during WWII. He manned one of his plane's .50 caliber machineguns to fend off marauding enemy fighter aircraft on missions over Europe. He's a survivor of "The Big Week" in February 1944 when allied airmen flew six rugged, deadly days of regular day and night bombing raids against German aircraft manufacturing bases, boring ahead through some of the heaviest and deadliest enemy air defense ever encountered. Those missions were a sobering experience for a young air-gunner who enlisted in the Army Air Corps in January 1941 at the tender age of 17.

After basic training at Lowry Air Force base in Denver, Colorado, Lucky was ordered to Will Rogers Field in Oklahoma to train on A-20 Havoc bombers. He later trained on B-17s at airfields in Texas and then headed for the European Theater of Operations aboard the luxury liner Queen Elizabeth which had been converted to a troopship. As a new waist gunner in the 339th Bomb Squadron, Lucky was part of the Mighty 8th Air Force commanded by air pioneer Lieutenant General Jimmy Doolittle. He was just in time for Operation Big Week and flew with his squadron as they helped to drop more than 10,000 tons of devastating high explosives on enemy targets deep in the German homeland. One of his most frightening missions was in March 1944 aboard the B-17 nicknamed "I Dood It." German fire shattered Lucky's aircraft so badly that the entire nose of the B-17 was shot off. The pilots brought the aircraft back safely with only one wounded crewman aboard but the temperature inside the crippled bomber dropped to a frigid 60 degrees below zero during the flight home.

Lucky got his licks in against the enemy on a mission over Berlin, where he was credited with shooting down a Messerschmitt Bf-109 from his position in the waist. After surviving all the combat missions in B-17s it would seem obvious how he came by the Lucky nickname. Not so, he says with a smile. It has to do with his narrow escape from court-martial for hitting an officer.

First Lieutenant Arthur Meyers USAAF
Navigator and Former Prisoner of War
705th Bomb Squadron, 446th Bombardment Group (Heavy)
8th U.S. Air Force

Arthur Meyers enlisted in the U.S. Army Air Corps the month after Pearl Harbor was attacked. After basic training, he was commissioned and sent for advanced flight training at airfields in Texas. He was eventually assigned as a navigator with the 446th Bomb Group based at Lowry Field, Colorado. The group, including Arthur's squadron, was sent to the European Theater of Operations in 1943 and assigned to the Mighty 8th Air Force, conducting bombing raids on enemy targets throughout the continent. As the man primarily responsible for directing his aircraft to targets, identifying those targets, and then getting everyone home without getting lost, Arthur was a critical asset on his bomber's aircrew. The navigator in a B-24 used a combination of dead reckoning, visible landmarks, radio, and celestial navigation to get his aircraft and crew to the target and back home safely. Arthur flew in the nose of a B-24 on missions against German targets including U-boat installations at Kiel, the seaport at Bremen, chemical plants and ball-bearing works near Berlin and many others.

He had only three more missions left to fly before he reached the magic number of 25 that would rotate him home when he was shot down and forced to parachute from his crippled Liberator. He spent the next year and a half as a German prisoner in a *Stalag Luft*—a German Prisoner of War Camp for allied airmen—in Germany.

Second Lieutenant Terence Messing USAAF
Bombardier and Former Prisoner of War
365th Bomb Squadron, 305th Bombardment Group (Heavy)
8th U.S. Air Force

Terence Messing enlisted in the U.S. Army Air Corps in January, 1942, and was trained at a number of bases to become a bombardier in B-17 Flying Fortress aircraft. He was sent overseas to join the Mighty 8th Air Force and began to fly combat missions over enemy targets in Europe. During these dangerous missions, everything depended upon the bombardier's ability to hit the target. Lt. Messing's main tool was the top-secret Norden bombsight. On a mission, the bombardier took control of the aircraft at the Initial Point when the bombing run began. From that point, the bombardier would fly the airplane through the bombsight linked to the autopilot on a straight and level course through flak and fighter attacks. Sitting behind the bombsight in the nose, he controlled the flight until bomb release.

After flying just a handful of missions with the 365th Bomb Squadron, Lieutenant Messing's B-17 was hit by flak and fatally crippled. The aircraft plunged 10,000 feet before he was able to bail out with the rest of the crew over enemy-occupied Holland. He was captured by the Dutch SS shortly after he landed and then paraded through a number of occupied towns with other American prisoners of war. He spent the remainder of the war as a prisoner in German *Stalag Luft* #1 on the Baltic Sea.

When Terry returned to Normandy, he was largely confined to a wheelchair due to injuries he sustained on his last parachute landing. While in the town of Ste-Mère-Église, the weather turned bone-chilling cold, and he began to shiver. Just then, the Star Spangled Banner began to play. He looked up with a huge smile and said, "Play Ball."

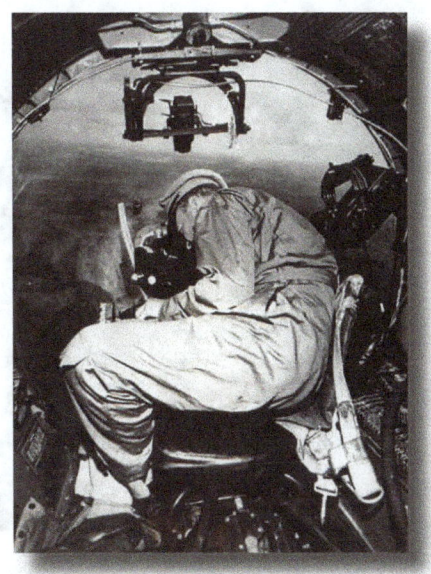

RETURN TO D-DAY

Technical Sergeant Frank E. Petrucci USAAF
Flight Engineer and Former Prisoner of War
508th Bomb Squadron, 351st Bombardment Group (Heavy)
8th U.S. Air Force

Frank Petrucci flew 29 bombing missions as a Flight Engineer on B-17 Flying Fortress aircraft over occupied Europe. His job on the aircraft was particularly important to the missions his squadron flew in World War II. The Flight Engineer was specially trained to know the B-17 from top to bottom with a wide knowledge of the aircraft and its systems. He was capable of servicing the aircraft if it landed away from its home base and he could perform most repairs normally handled by ground crews. He was also required to have a detailed knowledge of the aircraft's guns and bomb racks and was the go-to guy in any emergency situation.

Frank flew many of the pre-invasion missions designed to soften German defenses prior to June 6, 1944. He manned the B-17's top turret machinegun position and he was at that station during the saturation bombing of St-Lô shortly after the D-Day invasion. Frank returned to Normandy at age 92. Walking through the town of Ste-Mère-Église during the commemoration ceremonies, he took in the town's church and paratrooper memorials. Hundreds of people who had gathered for the ceremonies treated Frank and the other veterans like rock stars. They asked for his signature and took pictures with him, all the while thanking him profusely. He was calm throughout the hubbub, but later, at dinner, he became emotional thinking about his friends and comrades who had not survived—and would not be honored as he was.

RETURN TO D-DAY

Staff Sergeant Keith Hereford USAAF
Tail Gunner and Former Prisoner of War
365th Bomb Squadron, 305th Bombardment Group (Heavy)
8th U.S. Air Force

Keith Hereford enlisted in the U.S. Army Air Corps on Nov. 30, 1943. He underwent basic training in Amarillo, Texas and was then designated for training as an air gunner on bomber aircraft. He spent several months at various gunnery schools in California, Arizona, and South Dakota before he was shipped overseas to the European Theater of Operations. As a Staff Sergeant, Keith was assigned to fly in the tail gunner position on B-17 Flying Fortress aircraft. He joined the 365th Bomb Squadron and began flying missions to strike enemy targets deep in occupied territory.

His unit was involved in a number of crucial and very dangerous raids on heavy industry sites deep inside the German homeland. These missions always involved flying through some of the most intense and deadly flak and fighter concentrations of the war. Keith's unit was involved in the "Big Week" bombing raids on German aircraft industry targets in 1944. On his ninth combat mission, Keith's B-17 was shot down. He parachuted to safety but was captured and spent six months in a German POW Camp for allied airmen before the war ended.

First Lieutenant Thomas Kilker USAAF
Glider Pilot
437th Troop Carrier Group
Supporting the 82nd Airborne Division

Thomas enlisted in the U.S. Army in November 1943 from his hometown of Springfield, Massachusetts. After basic training, he was assigned to radio school and studied for duties involving combat communications. With the war action heating up in Europe and the Pacific, he volunteered for the new military glider program in June 1942. He was trained to fly the CG-4A Waco glider which was designed to carry infantry troops into combat after being towed behind a C-47 transport. When the tow aircraft got the gliders into position, they were cut loose and pilots like Thomas Kilker were then responsible for finding a landing area and guiding the unpowered glider to a safe landing which was more often a controlled crash.

Glider pilots were involved in D-Day operations from the first moments when they flew behind C-47s carrying paratroopers for the airborne assault on Normandy. During Operation Neptune, which was the airborne portion of the D-Day assault, glider pilots flew six separate missions carrying heavy equipment and supporting artillery for the airborne infantry. During one of these missions, Thomas Kilker piloted a Waco glider that landed at 4:10 a.m. on the morning of June 6, carrying the Jeep and driver for Major General Matthew Ridgway, the commander of the 82nd Airborne Division.

What he didn't know about his mission was that the landing area he selected for his glider was riddled with ruts, potholes and earthen banks that he could not see from the air. Tom did his best to wrestle the glider to a smooth landing, releasing a drag-chute on approach to slow his landing speed, but it was no help. The subsequent crack-up on the ground threw Tom clear of the aircraft and sent General Ridgway's Jeep hurtling from the cargo compartment and directly over him to crash on the muddy ground. Incredibly he was not injured in the crash or the near miss with the airborne Jeep. He made his way to cover in a nearby hedgerow as enemy artillery began to impact all around him. He made a forced transition from glider pilot to infantryman until he was finally sent back to England where he could get back behind the controls of yet another glider. After surviving combat in France, he also carried troops into combat for the allied Operation Market Garden landings in Holland later in 1944.

Thomas returned to Normandy for celebrations of the 65th Anniversary of the 501st PIR jump into France during World War II. His face lit up when he saw a reenactment of that event, complete with Jeeps, tents and paratroopers—so familiar to him from his wartime experiences.

RETURN TO D-DAY

Major John "Lucky" Luckadoo USAAF
Pilot
350 and 351st Bomb Squadrons, 100th Bombardment Group (Heavy)
8th U.S. Air Force

John Luckadoo entered active duty with the U.S. Army Air Corps in February 1942 at age 20. He went to basic pilot training and after receiving his wings was sent for advanced flight training in multi-engine aircraft at Valdosta, Georgia. He was assigned to the 100th Bombardment Group flying B-17 Flying Fortresses and shipped overseas for combat duty in May 1943. The "Bloody Hundredth," as the unit quickly became known, flew bombing missions from Thorpe Abbotts airfield in rural England while Lucky served as co-pilot, pilot and squadron operations officer at various times. The 100th suffered some of the heaviest losses in the ETO due to minimal fighter escorts on their long-range missions against enemy targets in Nazi-occupied Europe. On these missions they were always vulnerable to devastating antiaircraft fire and numerous encounters with highly experienced Luftwaffe fighter pilots. The inclement weather regularly encountered over England and Europe also added to the difficulty of flying combat missions.

In June 1943, Lucky flew his first combat mission to a target in LeMans, France but he didn't have much time to mark the event and his successful return to home base. Over the next eight months Lucky completed a combat tour of 25 missions and was returned to the United States in February 1944. He became an instructor for B-17 flight crews and was assigned to conduct combat crew replacement training at MacDill Army Airfield in Florida. While in this command, he was selected for transition training to B-29 Superfortress bombers. He qualified in the aircraft type and was preparing for further assignment to war in the Pacific when atomic bomb attacks on mainland Japan ended the war there. Lucky remained in the Air Force until 1948 when he resigned his commission as a Major. Using the GI Bill, he graduated from the University of Denver and became a commercial real estate developer.

During his return trip, Lucky placed a wreath at the base of the 351st Bomb Squadron's memorial with his friend Conrad Lohoefer, a fellow veteran of the 8th Air Force. Their common experience with the Flying Fortress gave them plenty to discuss, joke, and trade stories about "the most beautiful plane of the war."

Technical Sergeant Conrad Lohoefer USAAF
Flight Engineer
401st Bomb Squadron, 91st Bombardment Group (Heavy)
8th U.S. Air Force

Conrad Lohoefer was a flight engineer and top turret gunner on a B-17 Flying Fortress during World War II. After completing initial training at bases in Texas, Nevada, Nebraska and Tennessee, he was shipped overseas to join a combat squadron fighting the air war in the European Theater of Operations. He joined the 401st Bomb Squadron at Bassingbourne, England, just outside of Cambridge. His combat tour began almost immediately as the unit was heavily committed to striking enemy targets throughout enemy-occupied Europe. As a Flight Engineer, Conrad was the senior enlisted man on a bomber crew and responsible for as much maintenance as could be done while in flight. A lot of maintenance was often required when the B-17s ran into heavy flak concentrations and swarms of enemy fighters. Over a period of six months and 35 combat missions, Conrad did everything on his aircraft from hand-cranking shot-out landing gear and bomb bay doors to patching up wounded crewmen and fending off marauding fighters from his top-turret machinegun position.

He flew missions over heavily-defended targets such as Berlin, Dresden, Regensburg, Kassel, Cologne, Frankfort, Bremerhaven and many others with the 91st Bombardment Group which suffered the greatest number of losses of any heavy bomb group in World War II. On one of his missions to Germany, his aircraft was badly damaged and the crew was forced to make an emergency landing in Liege, Belgium where Conrad supervised the crew in repairing the aircraft so it could fly back to England. He finished his required combat missions and was on his way home before his 21st birthday. Through the GI Bill, he attended the University of Missouri and graduated in 1949 with a degree in journalism.

When Conrad returned to Normandy, he saw a piece of twisted metal that reminded him of the flak from German 88mm guns that exploded in the sky around him—looking like a bowl of burnt popcorn tossed into the air, the kernels suspended in the wind. On one mission in his B-17—known as "Old Battle Ax"—some of the aircraft systems malfunctioned. The pilot ordered him to get out of the turret and fix the problem. Having done so, he returned to the turret to find it had been blown apart. Later, the mechanic who had been fixing the aircraft came to him with the piece of shrapnel that had torn up the turret. That piece still sits in his den. He put the shrapnel in a shadow box with his wings and medals as a reminder. "Every time I look at it I shudder and remind myself how thankful I am to be alive."

Staff Sergeant Peter Bielskis USAAF
Ball Turret Gunner
546th Bomb Squadron, 384th Bombardment Group (Heavy)
8th U.S. Air Force

Peter Bielskis joined the Army Air Corps as a cadet at age 19 hoping to become a pilot. His grades in training didn't reach the required mark, but he still wanted to fly so he headed for training as an air-gunner. While he was qualified to man the machineguns at every position on a B-17, Peter took an unusual liking to flying in the ball-turret located on the belly of a Flying Fortress. Most of the gunners avoided this position as it was cramped and vulnerable to flak and fighter attacks from below a bomber formation, but Peter persisted and flew the position throughout his combat tour with the 546th Bomb Squadron flying from an airfield in England against targets in Nazi-occupied Europe. On his second mission his B-17 was shot-up badly and limping back across the English Channel on only one engine. The crewmen had to throw most of the guns and equipment out of the plane just to make it back home. On Peter's 21st mission over Germany, he encountered some German ME-262 fighters, the first jet-powered aircraft to enter the war.

Missions flown by the 384th Bombardment Group included attacks on enemy concentrations along the coast of Normandy prior to and during the invasion in June 1944. They also supported ground troops during the breakthrough at St-Lô by bombing enemy strong points just beyond Allied lines. The group hit tank and gun concentrations north of Eindhoven to assist the airborne assault on Holland during Operation Market Garden in September 1944 and struck enemy communications and fortifications during the Battle of the Bulge.

After completing his missions in Europe, Peter returned to the U.S. to train on the B-29 Superfortress after which he expected to be sent to the Pacific. The war ended before that happened and Peter was discharged in November 1945.

Peter didn't slow down after the war. Along with returning to Normandy to visit the sites of his missions, he took up parachute jumping, taking his first leap in 2013, at the age of 88.

RETURN TO D-DAY

Staff Sergeant Homer Goodman USAAF
Ball Turret Gunner
418th Bomb Squadron, 100th Bombardment Group (Heavy)
8th U.S. Air Force

Homer Goodman had a rather unpleasant birthday week in June of 1944. His eighteenth birthday was June 3 and three days later he was in a B-17 Flying Fortress on a bombing mission over the coast of Normandy supporting the landing forces on D-Day. Homer was the youngest combat crewman in the "Bloody Hundredth" Bomb Group flying B-17 Flying Fortresses out of Thorpe Abbots air base in rural England. As a ball turret gunner, Homer had one of the most dangerous positions on the aircraft. The ball turret was the only defense against fighter attacks coming at the B-17 from below where enemy fighter pilots knew the plane was most vulnerable. The ball turret was also very susceptible to flak damage from enemy anti-aircraft guns shooting up at the plane as it flew straight and level on bombing runs.

The 418th Bomb Squadron was involved in brutal aerial combat during the war. They flew strategic bombing missions over much of Europe sustaining very heavy losses in combat crews and aircraft. Most of their missions involved strikes on enemy airfields, industries, naval facilities, and transportation hubs. During 1944, aircrews bombed enemy positions at St-Lô in support of the Allied drive from the D-Day landing beaches. That was followed by other intense bombing missions to destroy German ground defenses during the Allied drive on the Siegfried Line.

On his 30th mission over enemy territory, Homer's B-17 was hit by clouds of enemy flak and was too badly damaged to continue flying. Homer and the rest of the crew had to bail out over enemy territory in Belgium. Using only his wits and survival skills, he managed to successfully evade capture for six weeks until he eventually returned to American lines during the Battle of the Bulge.

Homer enthusiastically told his story to the group on his return to Normandy. "Being back here is something I'll remember for the rest of my life," he said, fighting back tears. "This is where I lived. This is where I almost died. A lot of my friends almost died here."

Without missing a beat, he added, "A lot of them did die."

RETURN TO D-DAY

Captain Harold Steinberg USAAF
Pilot
386th Fighter Squadron, 365th Fighter Group
9th U.S. Air Force
IX Tactical Air Command

Harold "Heshie" Steinberg fought his share of World War II as a fighter pilot in the cockpit of a P-47 Thunderbolt. His squadron deployed from formation and training at Richmond Army Air Base, Virginia to England in December 1943 where they were assigned to the 9th Air Force, the command responsible for all fighter-bomber operations in the European Theater of Operations. Squadron pilots and ground crews trained for two months at Royal Air Force Base Gosfield before they flew the first combat mission in February 1944 escorting 8th Air Force heavy bombers on missions over Nazi-occupied Europe. Harold and other squadron P-47 pilots flew bomber escort missions until their mission was converted to fighter-bomber work in support of ground operations which was the type of mission they flew on D-Day. The Thunderbolt was a particularly good aircraft for ground support missions. It carried devastating firepower including eight .50 caliber machine guns, aerial rockets and two 1,000-pound bombs.

Heshie remembers being shaken from a sound sleep at 3:00 a.m. on June 6 to report for mission briefings. "This is it," the squadron commander told his pilots. "This is the invasion of Europe." Along with 35 other fighter pilots from his squadron Heshie was assigned to strafe the landing beaches in support of the infantry coming ashore. "All of the pilots wanted to be on that mission," he said. "It was monumental, something we'd never forget. We absolutely could not believe what we were seeing when we got over the invasion area." Heshie's squadron was sent against five separate enemy ground targets in Normandy on D-Day.

He continued to fly P-47s in mostly ground support missions as the Allies fought their way across Central Europe. Many times his squadron flew in support of General George S. Patton's rapidly advancing 3rd U.S. Army as tanks and infantry called on air strikes on enemy targets impeding their advance. The 368th Fighter Squadron was part of the first air group to move into Germany in 1945 at Aachen and the first to fly a combat mission off of German soil. They flew from missions from eleven air fields moving more times than any other fighter-bomber group in the 9th Air Force.

Heshie returned to Normandy in 2009. "I can't possibly express all the emotions, sadness, excitement, thanking God and the pride I felt for having had this trip and its memories," he said. "It was the most amazing experience of my life."

RETURN TO D-DAY
NAVAL SUPPORT:

As the bulk of D-Day landings were designed primarily as an assault from the sea, Allied naval forces played a pivotal role. Nearly 200,000 sailors from allied nations including the U.S., Britain, Canada, Netherlands, Norway, Poland, and Greece took part manning the ships of the invasion force. Some 7,000 ships supported the landings, including 1,200 warships firing support on targets ashore and 3,500 landing craft of all types which ferried men and supplies onto the Normandy beaches.

Petty Officer 2nd Class Joseph J. Scida USN
LCVP Crewman
LST 495, Flotilla 10, 60th Division
U.S. Navy Amphibious Forces

Joe Scida joined the Navy during World War II and was trained at Little Creek, Virginia and Fort Pierce, Florida as a crewman on an amphibious craft known as an LCVP or Landing Craft Vehicle and Personnel. These little troop and equipment transport vessels were usually carried into combat zones by larger vessels, especially an LST or Landing Ship, Tank. Joe found himself aboard just such a ship—LST 495—and headed across the Atlantic for England where hectic preparations were being made for the D-Day landings at Normandy scheduled for June 1944. As a crewman on a landing craft, Joe realized he would very soon be in the thick of the action when allied forces landed on the shores of Nazi-occupied Europe.

While training for the invasion, Joe's ship and his landing craft were involved in a tragic incident at Slapton Sands, an English beach where invasion ships and troops were training for the real thing. Some 300 men were killed in a combination of training miscues and live fire accidents. Joe nearly became a casualty himself during training in an experimental method of off-loading the smaller LCVPs from the mother ship. He survived the incident and was aboard LST 495 as she steamed off Omaha Beach on the morning of D-Day. When the command was given to land the landing force, Joe spent many nerve-jangling hours dodging enemy artillery and small arms fire as he ferried units of the 1st Infantry Division to the beach and carried casualties out to the ships for treatment. His landing craft was nearly hit by a German 88mm artillery round on D + 1 as he shuttled back and forth between Omaha Beach and the amphibious flotilla. He spent the next hectic week taking reinforcements ashore and hauling wounded and enemy prisoners out to the larger ships.

When Joe returned to Normandy, he located the gravesite of his good friend Karl, who served in the 8th Air Force and died on his fourth mission. He rushed over to it and knelt in front of the white cross, staring at his friend's name carved into the granite. Crossing himself, he stood to his feet and began talking about his friend. Although he missed Karl dearly, a peace settled into his eyes after at long last being able to say a final goodbye.

RETURN TO D-DAY

Seaman 1st Class William L. Brannan USN
LCVP Coxswain
60th Division
U.S. Navy Amphibious Forces

B ill Brannan began his World War II service by enlisting at age 16 in the U.S. Navy in December 1943. He was sent for basic training to the Navy Station at Farragut, Idaho and then selected for further training in amphibious operations. He took advanced training in various ships and landing craft at the Naval Base, Norfolk, Virginia where attended and graduated from a basic communications course. Like so many other amphibious sailors in early 1944, he was shipped across the Atlantic to join the armada building and training for the D-Day invasion of enemy-occupied Europe.

While in England, Bill also qualified as a Coxswain on LCVPs, the assault craft designed to shuttle troops and cargo from ships offshore to the Normandy invasion beaches. He was at the controls of an LCVP on the morning of D-Day. He spent that exhausting day and many others after the initial assault dodging enemy fire as his landing craft hauled assault soldiers into combat and evacuated wounded to the ships offshore for treatment. He survived the war and returned to those familiar Normandy beaches in 2009, where he walked up and down the sands, wondering how he and his fellow landing craft crewmen ever survived fire from the Germans dug in on the high ground above Utah and Omaha Beaches.

RETURN TO D-DAY
GROUND FORCES:

The most crucial element of the D-Day landings at Normandy was the assault by ground forces charging ashore on five designated beaches. The British landed on Sword and Gold Beaches, the Canadians came ashore at Juno and the Americans assaulted Omaha and Utah Beaches. There were some 160,000 troops involved in these amphibious landings against heavy German resistance. The initial American assault units in the first waves to come ashore included the 1st and 29th Infantry Divisions at Omaha Beach and the 4th Infantry Division at Utah Beach.

T/5 Donald Allen USA
Half-Track Crewman
Battery D, 195th Anti-Aircraft Battalion
2nd Armored Division
3rd U.S. Army

Donald Allen trained with his unit in California's Death Valley on the specially configured AA version of the U.S. Army's half-track and finished in time to ship with the battalion for service in the European Theater of Operations and the D-Day invasion. Donald's famous unit, known as "Hell On Wheels," landed shortly after the initial units attacked at Utah Beach and rapidly advanced as forces moved inland. His weapon was designed to provide anti-aircraft support for infantry units via quad-mounted .50 caliber machineguns and they traveled hard and fast to keep up with advancing elements of the 2nd Armored Division as they fought their way into Nazi-occupied Europe.

Donald was heavily engaged in the epic fight for Carentan on the Normandy battlefield where they supported paratroopers of the 101st Airborne Division. Using their heavy machineguns and mobility to knock-out enemy hard points, Donald and his fellow soldiers continued to battle furiously through the hedgerows leading to St-Lô and other critical objectives as allied units advanced from the landing beaches. He served with his battalion until the end of the war, with duty at one point as driver for his commanding officer. He served with occupation forces in Berlin after the official end of the war.

When Don learned about the trip back to Normandy, he said, "I'm ready to go! It's been 67 years since I've been there, and I'm ready to go back." When he stood on the beaches once again, he broke down, and could hardly bear the thought of remembering how many men died there. Driving through the French countryside, Don was overjoyed to discover American flags flown in private yards. He was as happy to see "Old Glory" flying at Omaha Beach as he ever was to see it in his homeland.

Private First Class Harry Dearwater USA
Wireman
116th Infantry, 29th Infantry Division
V Corps, First U.S. Army

Private First Class Harry Dearwater entered the European Theater of Operations as a replacement for hard-pressed units of the 116th Infantry, one of the lead elements of the 29th Infantry Division that landed at Omaha Beach on D-Day 1944. He was rapidly put to work running communication lines throughout the combat zone, very often under enemy fire. His mission was to maintain communications between the advancing infantry units and their artillery support.

He came ashore three days after the initial landings and fought to keep up with the infantry heading for St-Lô where he witnessed the hours-long artillery bombardment of that city prior to the attack that eventually took the crucial objective. Harry continued to keep artillery and infantry in wire contact until the battle for Brest, France where he was wounded in action. He spent time recuperating in various hospitals and returned to duty in time for General Patton's historic break out on the Normandy front. He was present with his outfit in January, 1945 when they liberated Paris and then fought with them all the way into Germany.

RETURN TO D-DAY

Private First Class Richard Lacey USA
Assistant Machinegunner
120th Infantry, 30th Infantry Division
First U.S. Army

After infantry training at Fort McClellan, Alabama, Private First Class Lacey shipped overseas and landed in France as a replacement in the 120th Infantry of the "Old Hickory" 30th Infantry Division on July 16, 1944. His unit was immediately engaged in break-out operations from the Normandy beachheads and he was engaged in combat as an assistant gunner on a .30 caliber machinegun firing support for rapidly advancing infantry. In July 1944, his unit was assigned to lead Operation Cobra, an effort to break out of the Normandy hedgerows. Due to a number of miscommunications, the 30th Division was hit by friendly fire from Army Air Force bombers attempting to carpet bomb a clear path for their advance. The unit suffered more than 100 casualties in this incident including their commander Lieutenant General Leslie McNair.

Richard fought with his unit during the drive to Avranches where they clashed violently with the German 1st SS Division. They continued to advance and were involved in the liberation of Paris. They drove across Belgium and fought their way into the Netherlands where they were involved in taking the heavily-defended city of Aachen. Richard carried his machinegun through all of these battles until he was eventually wounded and hospitalized. He recovered in time to rejoin the 30th Infantry Division for the infamous Battle of the Bulge. He was with his unit in Magdeburg, Germany when the war ended.

Richard loved returning to Normandy with students, saying they were "the great future of our nation." He was impressed by their interest in his war stories. "I hope that by sharing my successes and failures with these young, future leaders," he said, "I am preserving the legacy of love of country and the value of duty, honor, and sacrifice in defense of freedom."

RETURN TO D-DAY

Captain Malvin Walker USA
Platoon Leader
Company L, 115th Infantry, 29th Infantry Division
V Corps, First U.S. Army

Malvin Walker was inducted into the U.S. Army in July, 1942 and after basic training, he joined an elite unit of Army Rangers that was involved in formation of the 63rd Infantry Division. Like many other officers in that recently-activated division, Malvin was selected for immediate assignment overseas to one of the units preparing for Operation Overlord, the invasion of Nazi-occupied Europe at Normandy. As a Second Lieutenant, he became a Platoon Leader with Company L, 3rd Battalion of the 115th Infantry. His unit was part of the 29th Infantry Division slated to land on Omaha Beach against what was expected to be stiff resistance from the German 352nd Infantry Division. Omaha was known to be the most difficult of the five landing beaches, due to its rough terrain and bluffs overlooking the beach that had been heavily fortified by enemy defenders. Malvin led his platoon ashore on the morning of June 6 and immediately came under intense enemy fire.

After fighting their way off Omaha Beach, Malvin's unit immediately became involved in break-out operations designed to expand the beachheads and drive deeper into enemy-occupied France. The 29th Division was ordered to cross the Elle River and advance toward St-Lô which involved bitter fighting among the Normandy hedgerows. It was in those heavily-contested hedgerows—known as *bocage*—that Malvin was badly wounded. "They hit me in both arms and legs," he said. "One arm was hit twice." In the blaze of machinegun fire, his M-1 carbine was cut in half and one round lodged in a steel plate covering the Bible he always carried in his chest pocket.

He was evacuated to the 61st General Hospital where he spent three months recovering from his wounds. He rejoined his unit and fought with them across the continent until they eventually entered northern Germany and held at the Elbe River. As a Captain, Malvin was still serving with the 29th Infantry Division when the war ended.

His interest in World War II never waned. He authored the widely acclaimed "Chronological Encyclopedia of Adolf Hitler and the Third Reich." He was also an accomplished musician and composer, but Malvin was never pretentious or self-centered. When he finally returned to Normandy, the memories kept him mostly silent and introspective. He listened intently to his fellow veterans but hardly mentioned his own experiences.

Private First Class Alfonso Villa USA
Combat Engineer
237th Engineer Combat Battalion and 554th Engineer Heavy Pontoon Battalion
VII Corps

35 MEN, 70 LANDINGS AT NORMANDY

After completing basic training as an Army combat engineer in 1943, Alfonso Villa shipped out to North Africa where he spent time guarding enemy prisoners and allied equipment at military bases around Algiers and Casablanca. His unit of the 237th Combat Engineers was sent to England where hectic but top-secret preparations were underway for the invasion of Nazi-occupied Europe. As a skilled engineer and strong swimmer, Alfonso was selected for training in underwater demolition work. His duties included swimming toward enemy beaches and helping to destroy landing obstacles and fortifications to clear a path for the landing force. He underwent long, tough hours of training that mainly focused on typical German barriers and how to destroy them with various explosives devices and charges.

Alfonso was among the first allied soldiers to land at Omaha Beach on D-Day in June 1944. His mission was to push forward through intense enemy fire, locate obstacles and destroy them so the infantry and armor formations could move forward as rapidly as possible. He continued on this dangerous mission, working well ahead of the infantry he was assigned to support until the 237th Combat Engineers reached Carentan where he was badly wounded in an ear and eye by a close mortar detonation. He was evacuated back to Southampton, England where he could recover from his wounds at a military hospital. While in the hospital, he was awarded the Purple Heart by General Omar Bradley, commander of the U.S. First Army. It was a powerful moment for the young combat engineer and he is clearly moved in re-telling the story.

When he had fully recovered, Alfonso returned to the battle front and joined the 554th Engineer Heavy Pontoon Battalion, an outfit specially trained and equipped to construct bridges across Europe's many rivers and water obstacles for advancing infantry and armor units. This work was often accomplished well ahead of the battle lines and usually under heavy enemy fire. He remained with his bridging unit through the Battle of the Bulge and had advanced to just outside Berlin when the war ended.

It was hard for Al Villa to express himself when he returned to Omaha Beach after 68 years after the war, but words were superfluous standing on the same stretch of sand that he'd first seen on D-Day. His clear eyes and proud posture told his story and reflected the memories that were running through his mind.

RETURN TO D-DAY

Private Hardin Cooper USA
Ambulance Driver
Company B, 60th Medical Battalion, 6th Engineer Special Brigade
V Corps

When Hardin Cooper joined the Army in 1943, he was assigned to Company B of the 60th Medical Battalion. After completing basic and advanced training as an ambulance/truck driver he shipped out to England. His battalion was quickly involved in the top secret training and preparations for the D-Day landings. The 60th Medical Battalion was slated to come ashore in Normandy on June 6 and immediately begin medical support of the advancing infantry. In the late afternoon of D-Day, the first elements of the 60th Medical Battalion, as part of the 6th Engineer Special Brigade, landed on Omaha's Easy Green Beach. An attempt was made to clear this beach, but direct artillery and small arms fire forced the medics to move into a covered position above high water mark where they established a casualty collecting station. That's where Hardin joined his unit as he landed with the second wave on D + 1. He was staggered by the losses the assault infantry had suffered on Omaha Beach. The doctors and medics of his battalion were faced with nearly 1,500 dead and wounded that needed immediate treatment or evacuation.

While the rest of his unit and another medical battalion continued to land people and equipment on Omaha Beach, Hardin began transporting medical supplies and helping the medics in any way he could. He stayed with his unit, collecting casualties from various battlefields and transporting them for medical care, throughout the rest of the war. He finally made it home in January 1946.

When Hardin returned to Normandy in 2012 at age 90 he plodded on like the old soldier he was, showing the same resilience that carried him through World War II. Like many other returning veterans, Hardin showed a remarkable spark when the memories began to flood. After spending the night in a chateau that was once the headquarters of Field Marshall Montgomery, and quite sore from the previous day's outings, he insisted that nothing would stop him from seeing Omaha beach, the place where he helped evacuate so many wounded men on D-Day.

RETURN TO D-DAY

Sergeant William Simpkins USA
Platoon Sergeant
22nd Infantry, 4th Infantry Division
VII Corps

Bill Simpkins, a Nashville, Tennessee native, left for the European Theater of Operations with his regiment of the famed "Ivy Division" in January, 1944. The division was headed out of New York, across the Atlantic, and into combat for the D-Day landings. They didn't know all that at the time, but Bill and his fellow infantrymen were glad to get ashore near Plymouth, England and into camp where training began. After six months of hectic preparations, they were finally told about the invasion of Nazi-occupied Europe and their role in it as the primary landing force on Utah Beach.

The 22nd Infantry landed as a lead combat element of the U.S. VII Corps on the morning of June 6, 1944 with other units of the 4th Infantry Division. While enemy resistance was not as stiff as it was on nearby Omaha Beach, Bill Simpkins and his fellow infantrymen came under intense German artillery and small arms fire as they struggled to get ashore, get organized and get off the beach. By sundown on D-Day, the regiment had reached their first objective. They were then turned against determined enemy efforts to stop them and headed for Cherbourg, the key to Allied control of the Cotentin Peninsula. Allied planners badly needed this deep-water port to supply attacking units moving inland and Bill's unit was attached to the fast-moving 2nd Armored Division in the effort to capture it.

After Cherbourg was captured, Bill's regiment was returned to the 4th Infantry Division and headed across the continent as part of Operation Cobra, the massive push through German defenses to reach Belgium. Bill and his buddies fought through that engagement and forced their way into occupied Luxembourg. When the enemy was routed there, the 22nd Infantry moved into Belgium and fought there until January 1945 when they swept into the German homeland. Bill was with his unit there on mop-up operations and on occupation duty after the German surrender.

On his return trip to Normandy, Bill was able to find the same stretch of concrete seawall he'd used as cover from the intense enemy fire pouring down on Omaha Beach 65 years earlier.

RETURN TO D-DAY

Sergeant Austin Cox USA
Platoon Sergeant
115th Infantry, 29th Infantry Division
V Corps, First U.S. Army

Austin Cox, a native of Crisfield, Maryland, was an experienced infantryman and a trusted enlisted leader in his company of the 115th Infantry, but he'd never been through anything like the chaos on Omaha Beach on D-Day 1944. He led his platoon ashore in the early morning hours of June 6 against determined German defenders who fought back with intense small arms, mortar, and artillery fire. If that wasn't trouble enough for the landing force assigned to take the western sectors of Omaha, many of the assault elements were landed in the wrong places due to strong tides, enemy fire and misdirection in the confusion of combat. As one of two Regimental Combat Teams in the initial landings alongside the 1st Infantry Division, Austin's unit of the 29th Infantry Division suffered heavy casualties from German defenders dug into the bluffs overlooking the beach. Many of the officers and senior NCOs were killed or wounded early in the landing, and more junior men like Austin had to step up and take command.

After fighting their way off Omaha Beach and scrambling to reorganize, Austin's platoon immediately was assigned to assault and capture objectives inland. That involved intense, close-quarters fighting in the Normandy hedgerows. As with many other infantry veterans of D-Day operations, Austin believes Allied success on D-Day and thereafter should be credited to small unit leadership plus initiative and determination on the part of individual soldiers. He survived bitter combat all across central Europe and ended the war still serving with the 29th Infantry Division with which he earned a Bronze Star Medal plus four battle stars on his ETO campaign ribbon.

"I am so proud to be one of the few Citizen Soldiers left who belonged to the only National Guard Division—the 29th Infantry Division—to have landed on D-Day," Austin said. Looking back upon his return to Normandy, he said, "When thousands and thousands died every week, I wondered why it is I was blessed, unless I have to be the voice for those who are not here."

Technical Sergeant Buster Simmons USA
Medical Detachment
120th Infantry, 30th Infantry Division
XIX Corps, First U.S. Army

Buster Simmons arrived with his unit of the 120th Infantry in England in February 1944 following a long period of organizational training in the U.S. and a voyage across the Atlantic from the east coast. It quickly became obvious to Buster and his fellow infantrymen of the "Old Hickory" Division that they were being prepared for something big as they trained in the English countryside. All was revealed in the summer of that year when top-secret briefings began for Operation Overlord, the Allied invasion of Nazi-occupied Europe.

Buster's outfit came ashore at Omaha Beach on June 11, 1944 and was immediately assigned to relieve advancing elements of the initial D-Day assault force. The mission: To spearhead a break-out from the landing beaches and drive to St-Lô against stiffening German resistance. Buster and his unit then experienced one of the most devastating friendly fire incidents of World War II. The 30th Infantry Division was the spearhead of Operation Cobra, an effort to break out of the Normandy hedgerows. To support this push, Army Air Force bombers were assigned to carpet bomb a corridor for the 30th Infantry Division through enemy defenses. Through a maze of confusion and miscommunication, the bombs began falling on U.S. soldiers. The division on the ground suffered more than 100 casualties including its commander General Leslie McNair who was killed in the abortive attempt to kick-start Operation Cobra.

"You did not stop to think about how you would cope," he said. "You just did the best you could."

Buster survived and was with his unit when it clashed with the vaunted German 1st SS Division during the drive across France. The 30th Division is credited with stopping many major enemy counterattacks after the Normandy landings and was a spearhead in the Allied efforts to liberate Paris.

Buster was typically modest about his role during the D-Day landings and his subsequent service in the rest of World War II. He told a few stories, listened to a lot more, but the real impact of his journey back to Normandy was internal. Like so many others who get the rare opportunity to return to the scene of such a momentous event in which they played a part, he spent most of his time quietly remembering those who did not survive.

RETURN TO D-DAY

Staff Sergeant Raymond S. Schmitt USA
Squad Leader
137th Infantry, 35th Infantry Division
XV Corps, 3rd U.S. Army

Ray Schmitt was a citizen soldier with the 137th Infantry, a regiment of the Army National Guard's 35th Infantry Division composed of units from Kansas, Missouri and Nebraska, when his outfit was activated for service in World War II. The 35th Division immediately began an intense period of training before it was shipped overseas for service in the European Theater of Operations in May 1944. As a Staff Sergeant, Ray was with the 137th Infantry when it crossed Omaha Beach in July, a month after the bloody initial assaults on the Normandy coast. They were immediately committed to combat in the Allied effort to take the key French town of St-Lô against stiff enemy resistance. After helping to mop-up enemy hold-outs in the area surrounding St-Lô, Ray's unit drove enemy forces across the Cotentin Peninsula.

During their first month in combat, Ray and his fellow soldiers were heavily involved in brutal combat to clear the Normandy hedgerows of German defenders. The 35th Division is officially credited with repulsing 12 German counterattacks during this period. Ray and his fellow infantrymen fought all across the Normandy area and helped to push the German enemy back on a number of crucial fronts. They played a major role in the efforts to relieve surrounded American units at Bastogne during the Battle of the Bulge.

After a very fast and very brutal series of advances across central Europe, Ray and other soldiers of the 137th Infantry drove to the German border and crossed the Saar River in December 1944. It was a 295-mile dash that the division accomplished in just two days. The 35th Infantry Division helped to eliminate or capture enemy forces in Germany until April 1945, when the war ended. Ray was with his unit when it was sent to Hanover, Germany for occupation duty. He finally made it back home in September 1945.

Private First Class Dan Farley USA
Rifleman
A Company, 5th Ranger Battalion
Ranger Force C, V Corps

35 MEN, 70 LANDINGS AT NORMANDY

As a volunteer for service with the elite 5th Ranger Battalion, Dan Farley felt his training had made him as ready as he could be as he headed into Normandy on the morning of June 6, 1944. Everyone in A Company was thoroughly briefed on the Ranger mission but wind, weather, enemy action and the chaos of war required the Rangers to innovate as they stormed ashore on the Dog Green Sector of Omaha Beach. Farley was 17 then but he wasn't scared. "I was seasick," he said. "I just wanted off that damn boat."

Their immediate concern was to relieve a unit of the 29th Infantry Division that was pinned down by murderous machinegun and mortar fire from the heights above the beach. Using explosive Bangalore Torpedoes to blast a path through German beach obstacles, the Rangers advanced rapidly, forcing the Germans to deal with them and relieving the pressure on other assault units struggling to get off the beach.

Dan and 22 other Ranger survivors from his company headed for a rally point inland, fighting their way through enemy concentrations and capturing a bunch of German soldiers along the way. They were moving so rapidly that they eventually had to simply disarm the Germans and leave them behind for other units to handle. Near dark on D-Day, Dan and his fellow Rangers joined up with men from the 2nd Ranger Battalion and a couple of mis-dropped paratroopers from the 101st Airborne Division at Vierville. They defended that position against determined enemy counterattacks until morning. On June 9, Ray and his unit assaulted an enemy artillery battery at Grancamp-Maisy and overwhelmed the German SS troops defending it during an intense battle.

When the allied forces finally managed to break out of the Normandy beachheads, Dan and his fellow Rangers continued to fight their way through fierce enemy resistance as they pushed inland. Once France was cleared of German occupation, the 5th Battalion Rangers continued to lead the way in other brutal battles in the march across central Europe. Dan survived the fighting during the Battle of the Bulge and the close combat during the fighting for control of the Huertgen Forest. His unit was eventually attached to General George Patton's 3rd U.S. Army and helped to liberate prisoners in the enemy concentration camp at Buchenwald.

Like so many of his fellow veterans who managed to survive the bloody landings on Omaha Beach, Dan was glad to go back many years later and walk the sands. It looked much more peaceful than the first time he'd seen it on D-Day in 1944. "It all came back to me," he said. "I remember thinking about throwing a hand grenade that didn't go off…thinking about a guy in my company that got shot. It was emotional. You can't help but have tears."

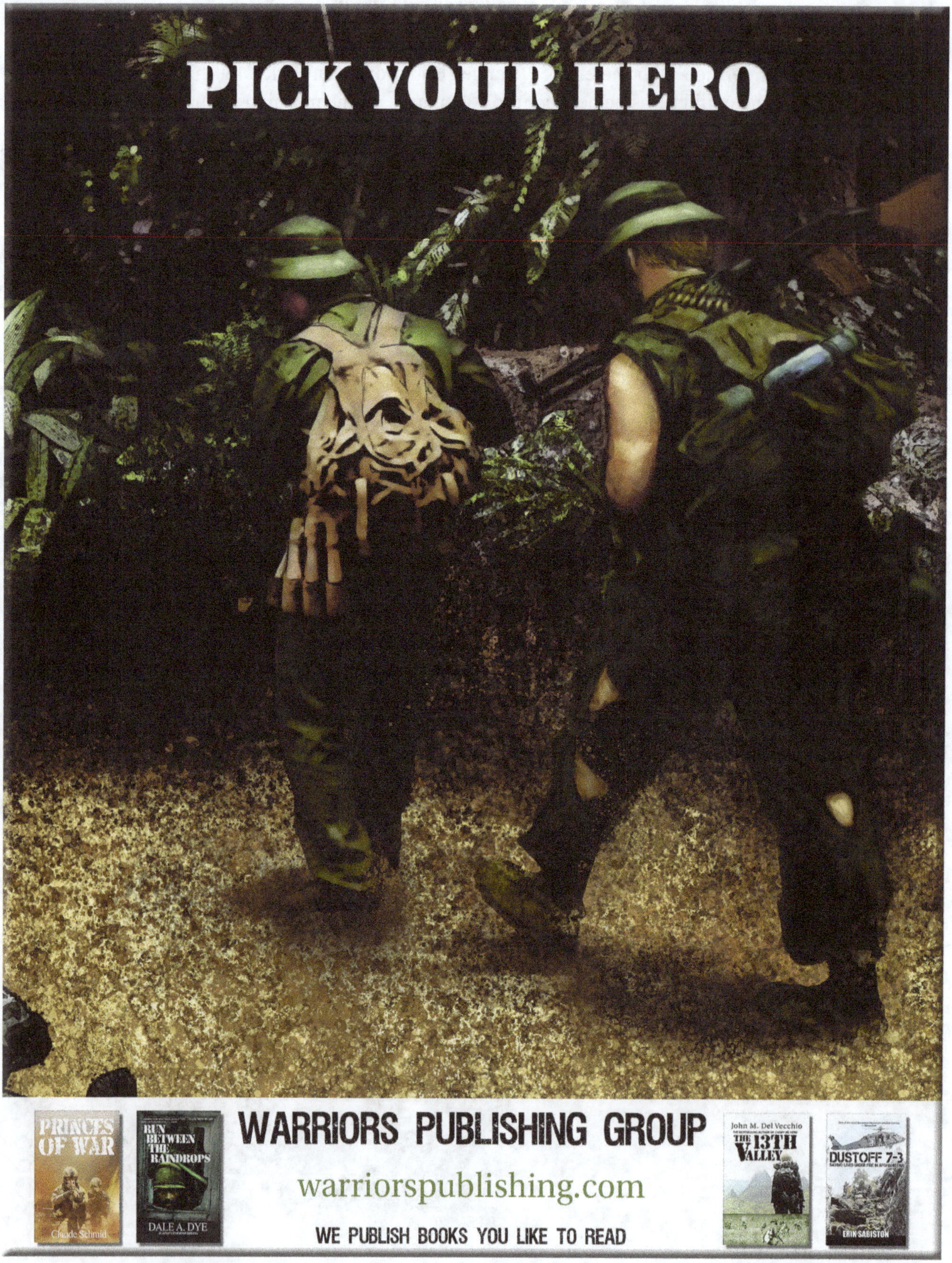

PICK YOUR HERO

WARRIORS PUBLISHING GROUP

warriorspublishing.com

WE PUBLISH BOOKS YOU LIKE TO READ

www.ingramcontent.com/pod-product-compliance
Lightning Source LLC
Chambersburg PA
CBHW081730100526
44591CB00016B/2566